Inflate Your Income

The Bounce House Business Booklet

By Jeremy Warlen

Contents

Introduction

Do you have extra time on your hands you want to use wisely and start working towards your financial freedom? Are you the kind of person who enjoys fun events? Well a bounce house business is a great opportunity for you then.

When people ask me, "why do you feel that a bounce house is a great investment?" I tell them, every day is another kid's birthday. So when you think of it like that, you then look past the silliness of a bounce house and you see the demand that they have. That demand is your potential profits. And believe me; the demand for bounce houses is real!

Another bonus about this business is it doesn't cost much to get started. And better yet, it doesn't take much too actually start making money. Depending on what style and size bounce house you decide to buy of course. But you can find a starter commercial bounce house with blowers for fewer than one thousand dollars. And the bigger inflatables are an average of five thousand or under.

If you feel like one thousand dollars is a lot and you still need a positive push to get into this business, then you will be happy to hear that these bounce houses rent anywhere form a hundred to a few hundred dollars for just one day. So with some word of mouth, you can easily make your initial investment back in the first year or earlier.

This business also has room for a lot of potential growth. You could just buy one to start with and do only as a side gig during the weekends, but you might see the demand in your area is high and start growing into a full time rental business by buying one or two more bounce houses when you can afford too. The greatest part is, most events are done in the evening or on the weekends so you don't have to quit your day job to make this work.

What to Look For

You need to find-

Commercial Grade Vinyl Inflatables.

Don't buy the small bounce houses they sell at your local superstore, those can't handle the rental game. Now that you know what material to look for, the style is truly just your preference. The styles and themes of bounce houses are endless. They have regular bounce houses, bounce houses with slides (most popular btw), huge 25 foot inflatable dry or water slides, Velcro walls, obstacle courses of any size and the list goes on and on. If you really feel like it, you can custom design your very own inflatable creation! But it will cost you a pretty penny. You can easily search "commercial grade bounce house for sale" on Google and find all types of cool inflatable companies to choose from.

Usually each commercial bounce house is sold with its very own blower. But if the one you have purchased didn't, you will need to check for the label stitched on the side of your bounce house; from there you should be able to figure out the size of the blower that house needs to be properly inflated. If not, you need to contact whoever you the bought bounce house from.

Other Things You Will Need-

- **Truck and/or Trailer** for hauling.

- **Long Nosed Hand-truck with Straps** to haul around the uninflated bounce house places you can't drive to.

- **Weights and/or stakes** to hold the bounce house down in place.
    - If you use weights, you will need bungee cords or rope to tie to the bounce house.
    - If you use stakes, you will need a mallet or sludge hammer to tamp into ground.

- **Utility Tarps** to go under your inflatable. This helps the wear and tear of the base of the inflatable. Also many events like tarps to be by the entry of the inflatable, that way people can take their shoes off and not be standing on the ground barefoot.

- **Extension Cords** of each size
    - 25 Foot
    - 50 Foot
    - 100 foot
        Bring all sizes to each event. You can never have too many cords. A lot of times people want the bounce house farther away from the outlet than they initially thought.

- **Gas Powered Generator**. You don't need this in the beginning if you can't afford it. But having this to offer is a win-win. The customer wins because they found someone who has the whole package for their event. Their event is in the middle of a field and no outlets are around. It's a win for you because you can upcharge the rental amount because now you are renting them the generator on top of the bounce house service. You will pay off you generator faster than you think, and you won't miss out on any event just because of an outlet. Once you buy the generator, I suggest you bring it to every single event in case of emergency. I have had people forget there wasn't an outlet close by and having that generator was a saving grace to them. They will pay the extra charge.

- **Storage.** You will need a safe place to store the bounce house when it's out of season.

- **Repair Kit**-
    - Vinyl Patches (same color as your bounce house)
    - Flexible Adhesive for Vinyl, Fabric & Plastic.
    - Duct Tape (same color as your bounce house)
    - Have an Upholster on call.

- **Cleaning Kit**-
    - Shop Vacuum
    - Towels & Rags
    - Water Hose

- Disinfectant Spray and a Wash Rag. Before using any cleaning agent, make sure all ingredients are safe to use and not harmful to skin contact.
- Lubricant Wax. If you have an inflatable that has a slide, use a lubricant wax after disinfecting to keep that area slippery. Before using any lubricant wax, make sure all ingredients are safe to use and not harmful to skin contact.

- **Water Hose.** You will need a water hose for your own cleaning but you might need extra water hoses if you rent out inflatable water slides.

Protect Yourself First

Before you rent out your bounce house, you will need to create an LLC (Limited Liability Company) and become an actual business. This will help protect your own personal finances if ever your bounce house business was to get sued. Also having it as an LLC, you can get some tax benefits.

Next we need to quickly discuss insurance. Insurance on this kind of business varies in different cities and states. A lot of people in this industry debate about whether or not to get insurance for their bounce house rental business. I suggest companies consider the following on whether or not to insure their bounce houses:

With Insurance:

- Security of protection against liability.

- Opportunity to rent at parks, recreation centers, and a lot of other event locations.

NO Insurance:

- High risk of losing business to a lawsuit.

- Limited to servicing "small" events.

Finally, even if you decide for some reason to not do the other two guidelines suggested before, you need to at least have a Rental Agreement already wrote up and ready before your first rental. This will help protect you in a court room. All a rental agreement is simply the signature of the person who is paying for the bounce house stating he/she is fully responsible for any accidents that may occur while in their possession. Accidents can happen on these bounce houses, so you need to protect yourself and make sure you are not responsible for any injuries.

The agreement is not only for possible accidents, it's also for damage control. If a hole is made or something somehow breaks during the time of their rental, they have to pay for the damages. That is what they have agreed too.

I suggest you do a walk around with the lessee in the beginning so they can see you are serious about this rule. Understand, the lessee will point out any flaw they see to you during this walk around, stay polite, they are just trying to not get swindled either. If they have deflated the bounce house by the time you shown up to pick it up, reflate it there to make sure they are not trying to hide any issues that may have occurred.

I also suggest you pay a lawyer in your area to write up the rental agreement for you so you are as safe as possible.

Pricing

You need to be competitively priced in this business because people will call you just to price check quite often. That just comes with this kind of business. They want to find an affordable cost so their kids can have fun yet they don't want it to break the bank.

So what I did when I first got interested in the bounce house business was call all my soon to be competitors before I even bought the bounce house. This would give me a good idea of where the market is, and where I could find my advantage. Also since I had already priced a bounce house, this gave me an idea of how many rentals I would need to get to pay off my investment and start making profit. Each competitor in my area was very close in cost and service. All were around $250 for one day rent. You had to pick up, set up, tear down and deliver back to them for this price.

You can decide to run your business that way if you want or you can go the direction I went; I had to stand out from the crowd so I undercut everyone in price by a hundred dollars and I actually brought a service to our area. I would deliver and pick it up. It only takes about 30 minutes in total of work (set up/tear down) and I make $150 on average. I have seen the prices go up to $375 for the same bounce house and service in bigger cities than mine; you just need to do some research in your area to see what your market price is. Here is some examples (all depending on size of course) of my rental rates but remember your market might be different! You hopefully could have the opportunity to make more money.

Full Day Rates

- Regular Bounce House- $100-200
- Bounce House with 1 Slide- $150-200
- Bounce House with more than one Slide- $200-250
- Obstacle Course- $150-300
- Big Inflatable Dry Slides- $150-275
- Water Slides- $175-225 (Water slides will be more work to tear down, so charge a little more.)
- Inflatable Velcro Walls- $200-300 (You have to provide the Velcro Suits and might have to stay to work the event so charge a little more.)

I also want to point out, you can decide to rent your products by the hour but I personally feel you will lose to your competitors with this plan. No one likes feeling like they have to watch the clock so why would they put themselves in that position? They won't.

Plus if you make them pay by the hour you won't get to charge as much and they will try to swindle you for just a couple hours. It's going to take the same amount of work to set-up and tear down so you might as well get paid correctly for it. Just make the rent one price. They will either pay for it or they won't.

On top of you initial price you can also make some extra money in the delivery charges. I offer free delivery within 20 miles, after those 20 miles I charge .75 cents per mile. Believe it or not, this extra income adds up fast. People love getting things for free, so when they see on your advertisement that you deliver for free within X amount of miles, that alone helps them pick up the phone and dial. People want to feel like they are getting the best deal possible. Make them feel like they did, and you will have return customers.

Another point on making customers feel like they are getting a great deal is you should offer **some** discounts. Since it is your business you can decide if you want to do this or not, but personally for me it seems to help out. The only discount I offer is $25 off to any School or Church event. This has had a huge impact on my revenue once I started doing this. Now, 75% of my bounce house income comes from School or Church events because I give them a deal on top of a good service.

Now, why I bolded out the word "some" above is because I don't want you to get carried away with discounts. In this business people will try to negotiate prices all the time. Stay firm on your prices and your discounts. Once word gets out that you gave Customer 2 a better deal than Customer 1, you just lost business and everyone will want Customer 2 price from now on. So figure out what your prices are and what discounts (if any) you want to offer and stay firm to them.

Side Note: School & Church events are more supervised than a regular backyard event so the wear and tear on your bounce house is way less. Also they normally don't last as long as a backyard event, so it's fast money.

Many people don't see an inflatable and think "Wow, there is a million dollar idea." But they don't know the demand these inflatables actually have. Have you ever been to an outdoor festival or a State Fair that has 10-30 inflatables all lined up? Well the person who rented those you can bet has a smile from ear to ear because he/she is getting paid the big bucks.

I have seen many times at my annual small hometown fair where they will have a company bring in around 10-12 inflatables for the kids to play on and that company charged $4000. This fair is only 3 nights long; each night is around 6 hours, so that's 18 total hours of work. That is $222.22 an hour for this particular event. The work is no more than turning on the inflatables, sitting in a chair in front of the inflatable and maybe taking tickets. Not the hardest job in the world to make that kind of money in that short period of time.

I have seen bigger events with 30+ inflatables go for upwards of $10,000 for a weekend of work. It's insane when you can find the right clients! The best part is the guy who is making $10,000 in a weekend started with only 1 bounce house just like you. The money is out there. Start small and work your way up. This can be just a side hustle or it can be a full time job, it's all up to you.

So for fun, I added a chart on the next page of how many rentals you will need to hit the magic number of 1 Million dollars.

I hope you all hit that magic number someday!

How Many Rentals You Need To Make 1 Million Dollars

$100 Rent x 10,000 Rentals = $1 Million

$200 Rent x 5,000 Rentals = $1 Million

$300 Rent x 3,334 Rentals = $1 Million

$400 Rent x 2,500 Rentals = $1 Million

$500 Rent x 2000 Rentals = $1 Million

$1000 Rent x 1000 Rentals = $1 Million

$2000 Rent x 500 Rentals = $1 Million

$3000 Rent x 334 Rentals = $1 Million

$4000 Rent x 250 Rentals = $1 Million

$5000 Rent x 200 Rentals = $1 Million

$10,000 Rent x 100 Rentals = $1 Million

Marketing

Word of Mouth-

This is your bread and butter in the Party Rental World. People talk at parties and then people leave and talk about other people's parties. Word of mouth is can make you king of your local industry or can kill your business. You need to make this part of marketing work in your favor.

The bounce house is a giant conversation piece. People will talk about it, guaranteed. Especially if the other people at the party have children of their own, so this being said, you need to have great customer service skills. You need to always have a smile on your face, be polite, and be professional. What I mean by *be professional* is- KNOW YOUR STUFF.

Most of the times at backyard events (especially if this is the customers first time ever renting a bounce house) the parents will come out and bombard you with questions the entire time you are setting up. This will be something you will just have to get use too. You have to remember, not everyone owns a bounce house, so the things you may think as "common sense" the customer may not see it that way. They are just asking these questions for the sake of their child's safety so you have to look at it that way. Just be polite and answer everything to the best of your knowledge.

Things to know from common questions:

- Size of your bounce house. Length, Width and Height.
- Weight Restrictions. Your bounce house should say somewhere (usually on front label) the total weight it can handle. Then you divide that by the number of children they plan of having at the party. This will give you an educated guess on how many kids are allowed in at one time. They pay attention to this rule because you had them sign the rental agreement stating they will fix it if it breaks during their time rented.
- Shoes allowed or not allowed? (Up to you.)
- How the bounce house operates. Most renters want to know how they can inflate and deflate the bounce house so

they can do it at the correct time and not waste too much of their electricity.

- Can adults jump? The most common question. They usually say it as a joke so act like you haven't heard it before and refer them back to the total weight restriction. Let them know you don't mind if they jump as long as they are mindful of the weight. Letting them feel allowed to play in it seems to always give them a smile. Adults want to play too, so let them and you will have return customers.

Sign at Event-

Every event I go to I bring a simple (but professionally made) yard sign that says- "Want this Bounce House? Call XXX-XXXX." That simple sign gets me attention from the people who might be too shy to ask the host where he/she may have got the bounce house. When their kid comes out of the bounce house and tells them "I want a bounce house for my birthday!" this sign is here for them to make that possible.

Be sure to have this sign before you start renting. You want people to know where they too can get in touch with your business. 99% of the time you aren't invited to the actual party, you are only there to set up and tear down. That sign does the work for you.

Make sure you are allowed to put it out though; I have had people get upset because I was "soliciting" at their event without permission. I haven't got called back to those events either for that reason. Sounds silly I know, but you have to be mindful of their rules, they are the ones paying you after all and you don't want to miss out on future events. Plus it's polite to ask for persimmon and most everyone will allow you too.

Business Cards-

This is a must for almost every business and bounce houses are no exception. You need a professional but fun business card.

Remember you are in the Party
Entertainment business now so you don't
want a boring business card. Make it loud
and colorful but have the information easy
to read and to the point. Pass them out
every time you set up at an event. Give the
host a few to give out to their friends. I
have made a ton of rentals because their
friend gave them my card. This easy
method works!

Flyers-

Just like business cards, your flyers need
to catch a person's eye but be easy to read
(no crazy font) and be straight to the point.
You can put more information on your
flyers than you can your business cards so
use that to your advantage. Put your prices
or deals on these flyers so people know
what they are calling for. You see, a lot of
times in this industry people will call you to
just ask prices and common questions.
While using a flyer, you can put all that
information on it so you don't have to
waste any of your time with those kinds of

phone calls. They will call you already knowing what they are getting.

Website-

You need a website for the obvious reason of being found through search engines like Google. Tons of people go to Google and just type in *Bounce House Rental Near Me.* If you don't have a website, it's likely you just missed out on that rental. With the world being the way it is today, you need to pop up in those search engines to stay alive.

It's cheap and easier than ever to create a website these days too. You can search for your domain name on sites like GoDaddy.com. Then once you buy the domain name you want, you can build a website easily on platforms like Wix or Wordpress.com.

Another reason having a website is a great tool is you have the power to collect emails. You can set up your website with a pop-up or side bar banner that has the option for the customer to get on your email list. You will most likely need to offer a deal to be able to collect their email initially. For example, you could say something like "Sign-up for our email list and save $25 on your next rental."

Collecting emails is huge because you can send out deals to your list to entice them to want to keep renting from you. This allows you to be able to RE-MARKET to them over and over. Returning customers is what you should always shoot for.

You can create mass email list through platforms like Mailchimp or ConstantContact.com

Facebook Page-

Making a Facebook Page for your business is almost as good as word of mouth these days. People will *Like* and *Share* your post, giving you attention from all of their friends and it just keeps going. This has been a huge help for me since I started 7 years ago.

I used to get more phone calls than Facebook messages, and then it turned to about 50-50. In 2017, I would say I got 40% rentals from phone calls and 60% rentals from Facebook Messages. So I would say having a Facebook Page is a must!

Facebook Page Reviews-

Reviews are huge for your business! Ask every customer you have to leave a review on your Facebook page. People look at reviews religiously before they will call you. So the more 5 star reviews, the more your phone will be ringing.

Thank You & Reminder Cards-

Making your customer feel like the most important customer is the key to your success. You should keep everyone's address in a customer database (Page 31) and send out thank you cards or reminder postcards to them. A thank you card should be written in hand to feel more personal, and should be sent out 1 week after their event is done. A postcard is cheaper than a letter and you can make them colorful and more fun looking. So I would recommend making business postcards to send out.

A reminder card is simply a marketing post card that is sent at the right time. For example- If you rented out an inflatable to John Smith in September last year for his daughter Emily's birthday party. You would send John a postcard early August saying something along the lines of-"Emily's Birthday is coming up soon. Let's make a date! Happy Birthday Emily! Talk soon."

Both Thank You & Reminder Cards are simple yet very effective at gaining return customers.

Create a Customer Database

Keep track of your customers in a simple database. You can create a simple database using Microsoft Excel or Access. You need to categorize each customer by month rented. This will help smooth along the process of sending out reminder cards the following year (Page 29). Getting personal reminders will make the customer feel special and will improve your odds of getting them to rent again. It will also help "Word of mouth marketing," because when they feel special, they will tell everyone.

Add the following information to your database-

1. Month & Date of rental
2. Customer name (Include spouse name if possible)
3. Customer Address
4. Customer Phone Number
5. Inflatable Rented
6. Children's Names
7. Children's Birthdays

The Phone Call

I'm not going to have a section on Facebook messaging because I am 99% certain you can do that with no training from me. But you can add these questions into the email if you like. I wanted to touch base on how to make an effective phone call.

First off always answer with a friendly voice and really put off the vibe you are willing to do anything you can to help this customer. Don't forget to sound confident. The best way to sound confident is to know your business inside and out. Refer back to "Common Questions" on page 22 and learn those answers then you will sound more confident.

To help smooth along the process of the phone call, I have wrote down a few questions I ask the potential customer to get all the information I need to bring a valuable service with no hiccups. Here they are-

1. What is the Date & Time?
2. What is the address? Does it show up on GPS?

3. Is this a good number to contact you if needed?
4. Do you have a level area that could fit a (enter your size) inflatable?
5. Is this level area on grass, gravel or cement? (That tells you if you need extra tarps.)
6. Is there an outlet nearby? If so, how far away do you think it is? If not, do you need to rent a generator for power?
7. (WATER SLIDES ONLY) How far away is the closest water spigot? (This tells you if you need extra hose.)

This should do it on information you need up front. If not, you always have a good contact number you can call back.

Here is an easy to use form on the next page-

Delivery Order Form

Event Date:	
Event Times:	
Which Inflatable?	
Customer Name:	
Event Address:	
Contact Phone 1:	
Contact Phone 2:	
Event Area?	☐ Grass ☐ Gravel ☐ Cement/Asphalt ☐ Other
Outlets nearby?	☐ Yes ☐ No
Other Notes:	

The Set-Up

When you first arrive to the event, try to be there early. Being there early will give you time to set-up and not be rushed and also gives you time to connect with the customer. Have a few laughs with them if possible; remember you want them to want to call you back. While talking with them, let them know you cannot set anything up without the Rental Agreement being signed. I also don't set-up till I'm paid, you can choose to do so before or after event. Once they sign the agreement and possibly pay you, you get to work setting it up.

The Set-Up is easy. You park your truck/trailer as close as you can to the desired spot for the inflatable. Then you haul the rolled up inflatable using your Long Nosed Hand Truck to the actual location the customer wants it set up. Roll it out, weight/stake it down, hook it up to the blower, turn blower on and walk away.

Here is where you will do your first walk around to see any issues your bounce house might have before this rental occurs. This is so you know if they have damaged it when you come back to check after the event is over.

Some companies like to do the walk around with the customer so they too can see any spots the inflatable might have an issue. When they are done with the walk around they usually have the customer sign an agreement stating they walked around and seen no damages. This is not needed if you already have the Rental Agreement signed, but it's keeping you safe two times as much so you might want to think about it. With the Rental Agreement you have the customer saying he/she will pay for damages if any occur and now also with the Observation Agreement saying he/she does not see any damages before the time of their rental.

The Tear Down

Before you tear down the inflatable you had just rented, be sure to do a final walk around while it's still inflated in place to check to see if any damages had occurred. Noticing this while still on the customer's property will be easier to confront them about the issue and get it resolved. If you take the bounce house home and notice the damage later, it will be hard to prove that they damaged it and not you. So I can't stress this enough, DO YOUR WALK AROUNDS!

When you first get your brand new inflatable, you need to set it up and tear it down in your own space as "practice" to figure out what is the most effective and timely way to set up and tear down. These inflatables are heavy and awkward to carry when deflated so you need to be aware of this to look professional when in front of your customers. You don't want to look like you are having a hard time. They are paying you for this service so that means they don't want to help you so don't make them feel like they need to. If they feel like they needed to help you, you probably just lost a future return customer.

So when you first receive your bounce house, you should pay close attention to the way the company has it rolled up to ship to you. They have it rolled as tight as possible which will be the best way you can roll it. The tighter its rolled, the less space it is taking up. Less space is important, especially when you start getting more inflatables in storage. So be sure to practice rolling it up before you rent it.

Side Note: Always be marketing! I notice at almost every tear down I do, I have someone come by to chat with me. Usually they are just curious about the Bounce House Business. This is an opportune time to pass out your business cards and sell your services.

Cleaning Your Inflatable

       This is the least fun part about this business but it has to be done. You need to clean your inflatables after each rental. Remember these inflatables are for kids; and kids have little hands filled with germs. You don't want to spread germs to anyone, because that's wrong and that is very horrible Word of Mouth Marketing. So make a habit of cleaning the inflatable after each use.

Here is a step by step way to clean-

1. Set-up and inflate your bounce house.
2. Vacuum the surfaces and inside each of the creases of the inflatable.
3. Rinse the entire inflatable with a water hose. Spray any mud clumps or debris off the inflatable.
4. Let it dry completely.
5. Spray the entire inflatable down with disinfectant spray and wipe with a wash rag. Make sure the disinfectant is not harmful to skin.
6. If you have slide, you will need to spray a lubricant wax on the slippery surface

after you have disinfected it. Be sure
the lubricant wax is not harmful to skin.
7. Leave it inflated and let the inflatable
completely dry before rolling back up.

Other Money Making Ideas

I decided to put this section in as a bonus. Once you start renting out inflatables yourself I am sure you will get the same kind of questions. People want the whole package and are usually willing to pay for it. So that being said here are the other things I frequently get asked if I have for rent along with the inflatable. Hopefully this sparks some interest and you go out and make more money! Good luck to you and thanks for reading this book.

Other Items You Can Rent.

- Gas Powered Generator
- Tables & Chairs
- Table Cloths, Chair Covers & Center Piece Decorations
- Popcorn Machine with Supplies
- Cotton Candy Machine with Supplies
- Snow Cone Machine with Supplies
- Hot Dog Cart with Supplies
- Helium Balloon Tank & Balloons
- Photo Booth with Supplies
- Selfie Booth with Supplies

- Red Carpet Runner
- Barricades & Stanchion Post with Rope
- Cool Backdrops for Red Carpet
- Ceremony Giant Scissors
- Volley Ball Net
- Basketball Hoop
- Rock Wall
- Raffle Drum
- Dunk Tank
- Corn Hole Game
- Human Sack Race Sacks
- Mechanical Bull
- T-Rex Inflatable Costume
- Inflatable Human Bumper Ball Suits
- Laser Tag Game
- Paintball Guns with Supplies
- Straw Bails
- Event Tents
- Event Tent Dance Floors
- DJ the Event (Added Service)
- Special Effects Light System
- Outdoor Speakers with PA System
- Karaoke System
- Bullhorns
- Video Projector
- Crazy Arms Dancing Man
- Portable Restrooms (Added Service)

Hope You Enjoyed This Book!

Yes... We have come to the end of this short booklet. I am so glad you stayed tuned and learned some valuable tips of this trade to help you steer onto the path of success.

I want to thank you for picking up this book. It truly means a lot to me.

Please leave an honest review on Amazon.

If you want to know more about me or my upcoming projects, go check out www.retirebeforeyourparents.com

Thank You!

-Jeremy Warlen

ISBN-13: 978-1985166219

ISBN-10: 1985166216

47